OWLS
AND
BIRDS OF PREY

LONGMAN NATURE LIBRARY

OWLS
AND
BIRDS OF PREY

Longman

Longman Group Limited
Longman House, Burnt Mill, Harlow,
Essex CM20 2JE, England
and Associated Companies throughout the world.

First published 1985

British Library Cataloguing in Publication Data
Owls and birds of prey. — (Longman nature library)
1. Owls   2. Birds of prey
598.9   QL696.F3

ISBN 0-582-89215-5

Colour illustrations © Marshall Editions Ltd. 1985.

Edited and designed by Curtis Garratt Limited
The Old Vicarage, Horton cum Studley
Oxford OX9 1BT

Set in MCS 9/10 pt Mallard

Printed in Spain
by TONSA, San Sebastian

CONTENTS

INTRODUCTION

Imagine yourself running as fast as you can towards a brick wall and then, just as you reach it, hitting the wall with your fist with all your might. This is the picture that the well-known authority on birds of prey, the late Dr Leslie Brown, once conjured to describe the power with which a peregrine falcon dives, or stoops, to attack its quarry on the wing. Birdwatchers around the world become interested in various different bird groups from the exotic birds of paradise to the humble but intriguing warblers. Few, however, could fail to be impressed by the speed of that peregrine's stoop, to be enthralled by the size and majesty of the California condor, or to be fascinated by the beautiful snowy owl. But these are just three of the nearly 450 species of exceptional and marvellous creatures that together are known as the birds of prey.

Birds of prey exhibit a full range of forms, sizes, colours, and habits, and occupy a wide variety of habitats. For instance, the peregrine, a falcon, is a medium-sized greyish bird with a streamlined body and pointed wings and preys mainly on other birds; the spectacular California condor, a type of New World vulture, is a huge, dark, powerfully built bird and feeds on carrion; while the snowy owl is a largish, white-feathered bird that hunts mammals and birds. And, when we consider all the other species of birds of prey, including raptors, as they are sometimes called, such as the hawks and eagles, the osprey and secretary bird, together with the bay and barn owls, the variety is even further increased. Within the groups, however, common features and resemblances can be recognized. Most of the species have large hook shaped bills, which are ideally suited to tearing flesh. Many have powerful taloned feet with which to kill and grasp their prey. Nearly all have particularly well-developed senses with which to hunt or find food. Thus the hawks, falcons, and eagles have keen eyesight, the night-time hunters, the owls, have good hearing as well as vision, and the vultures probably have a good sense of smell for locating their food.

This book deals with the two groups of birds of prey, the day-flying, or diurnal birds of prey, which include the vultures, falcons, eagles, hawks, secretary bird, and osprey, and the nocturnal birds of prey, which include the bay and barn owls and the typical, or true, owls.

There is a bewildering array of living things occupying planet Earth and, for a better understanding of the living world, scientists have found it convenient to divide this wealth of life into different groups of various sizes. The process by which these scientists, known as taxonomists, classify animals and plants is a complex and exacting one. And, as more and more is revealed about anatomy, physiology, and ecology, and as new animals and plants are discovered, the classification of the world's life forms must be constantly modified. It was once thought that all living things could simply be divided into two major kingdoms - animals and plants. Most modern systems, however, suggest that there may be as many as five kingdoms. These divisions are decided upon on the basis of many factors, such as the level of organization of the life form and the various ways in which it feeds and provides itself with energy for growth, maintenance, and reproduction. Whatever system is used, however, an animal kingdom is always recognized and this can be our starting point when we look at the classification of the two groups of birds of prey which are the subject of this book.

The animal kingdom is divided into a number of major groups called 'phyla' (singular 'phylum'). The phylum known as Chordata contains all the animals, such as fishes, amphibians, birds, reptiles, and mammals, that are characterized by possessing a flexible supporting rod in the body at some stage of their life. The members of this phylum which have feathers, scaly legs, a horny bill, lay shelled eggs, and are often adapted for flying are all grouped together into the 'class' Aves, or the birds. The birds are further divided into a number of 'orders', such as the Strigiformes (owls) and Falconiformes (eagles, hawks, falcons, kites, vultures) and each order includes a number of related 'families'. For example, the barn owls and bay owls belong to the family Tytonidae, while all the falcons are included in the family Falconidae.

People often wonder why taxonomists have to give living things seemingly difficult names consisting of two latinized words, conventionally printed in italics. For example, why should a barn owl be called *Tyto alba*, rather than simply a barn owl? In the eighteenth century, it was the intention of the Swedish naturalist, Carolus Linnaeus, to give every living thing a unique scientific name and it is on his original work that our present system is based. A major advantage of this is that a bird which in English is called a kestrel, in French a *faucon crecerelle*, in German a *turmfalke*, and so on, can be known internationally as *Falco tinnunculus*. The two words also give an indication of the origins, form, and relationships of this bird.

Looking at the scientific name, the falcons included in the family Falconidae, such as the hobby, gyrfalcon, and peregrine belong to the 'genus' *Falco,* but only the kestrel, which is a clearly separate 'species', is called *Falco tinnunculus.* The word *'tinnunculus'* is the species name and it is the species which is the basic unit of classification. It is, however, hard to define what constitutes a species and the reasons are beyond the scope of this book. An example must suffice: there is a number of barn owls belonging to the genus *Tyto* but only one barn owl, *Tyto alba,* which is different in many respects from *Tyto capensis,* the grass owl, and, indeed, from every other barn owl. Interestingly, the Strigiformes are more closely related to nightjars and cuckoos than to the Falconiformes which are classified between ducks and gamebirds, but both groups of birds have evolved as daytime and night-time hunters. These two unrelated groups of birds of prey have evolved their similar features in response to the parallels in their ways of life.

Both owls and the diurnal birds of prey are distributed throughout every continent of the world, with the exception of Antarctica, and occupy virtually every type of habitat from the densest tropical jungle to arctic steppes and dry deserts. They are the ultimate bird predators, interlocking and overlapping their hunting times to feed round the clock on a wide variety of food from snakes to bats, birds to fishes, and from insects to rotting carcasses. They range in size from the tiny, sparrow-sized elf owl and the little falconets to the huge eagle owl and the great and rare California condor, one of the world's largest flying birds. They may nest in the abandoned burrows of prairie dogs, in woodpecker holes, in trees, on the ground, in great stick eyries which

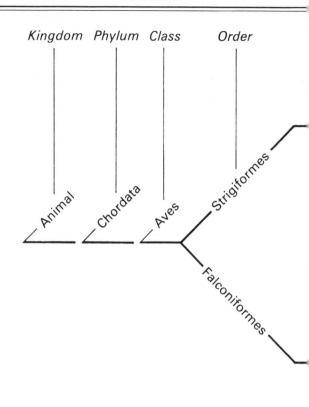

Classification of Birds of Prey and Owls

Family

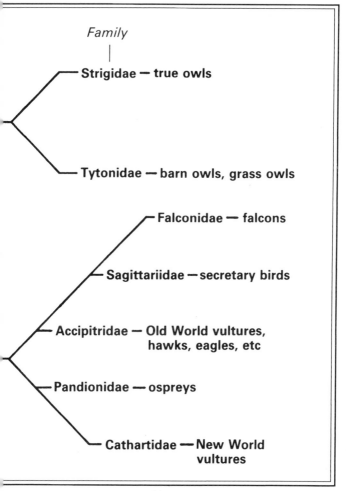

Strigidae — true owls

Tytonidae — barn owls, grass owls

Falconidae — falcons

Sagittariidae — secretary birds

Accipitridae — Old World vultures, hawks, eagles, etc

Pandionidae — ospreys

Cathartidae — New World vultures

are added to each year, on or in buildings, or they may build no nest at all.

Their anatomy is well adapted to their varying life styles. Although owls rely heavily on their sense of hearing for finding moving prey, their vision at night is exceptional - it is known, for example, that a barn owl can see a vole even on the darkest of nights. The eyes of owls are large and tubular in shape, forward facing, and very sensitive even at extremely low light levels. Because they occupy so much of the bird's skull, they cannot move far in their sockets. To make up for this, the owl's neck has extra bones and is very flexible - the bird seems to be able to look over its own shoulder without moving its body.

Hunting largely in the silence of the night as they do, it is vital that owls should not be heard by their potential victims. If you have ever heard a pigeon taking off, you will realize that its flight, as with most birds, is hardly noiseless. Owls, on the other hand, have one remarkable feature which enables them to fly quietly. The surfaces of their wings are soft and velvety while the edges of the flight feathers have soft fringes. These adaptations damp down the sound of the air which passes over the bird as it flies, although it does also mean that owls are slightly less efficient fliers than other birds with the more usual 'hard' feathers.

Most carrion-eating vultures have bald heads and necks. If they were feathered, they would soon become a sticky, bloody, and diseased mess as the birds delve deep into the insides of carcasses. These birds, too, have huge broad wings enabling them to rise on thermals and soar high in the sky with scarcely a beat of the wings as they range over the countryside in search of a meal. The forest owls and raptors tend to have short wings and long tails with which they can fly rapidly and with great manoeuvrability through the densely packed trees. The fish and sea eagles, on the other hand, have very short tails because they hardly need high degrees of manoeuvrability over their open hunting areas. And the wings of the fast-diving falcons tend to be long and pointed.

Few birds of prey use their legs much for walking but the secretary bird, which walks long distances every day and even kills prey by stamping on it, has very long legs ending in short toes. The unique burrowing owl is another long-legged species, using its long legs to escape to cover when disturbed. The feet of most birds of prey are specialized for killing, though not in the case of the vultures where the birds are adapted to feeding on carcasses. The osprey's foot is specially adapted to kill and grasp its slippery prey of fish. It has a reversible outer toe, which is helpful in carrying the fish, while the bottoms of its feet are covered with sharp spicules for extra grip.

Birds of prey have often found themselves at odds with humans. For example, until only a few years ago, the peregrine falcon was declining rapidly in numbers in many parts of its range. Eventually, it was realized that the bird's increasing scarcity was brought about by the collection of eggs by unscrupulous falconers and by the widespread use of certain pesticides. The falcons were concentrating these pesticides in their bodies and this caused them to lay eggs with progressively thinner and thinner shells which were easily broken before hatching could occur. Golden eagles were killed mercilessly in places such as Scotland because it was thought that they killed too many lambs. Many nesting birds were, and still are, disturbed unwittingly by those country lovers, climbers, or photographers who venture too close to the nest at breeding time causing the birds to desert.

Perhaps the most dangerous threat to the survival of all these magnificent and fascinating birds is the destruction of their habitat. Throughout the world, with the ever-increasing demands placed upon the countryside for housing, fuel, and farmland, forests are felled on a massive scale, deserts are greened, or wetlands are drained. The Mauritius kestrel, for example, may now be down to less than ten birds in the wild as the forest on its island home has been cleared. On this island, too, at least two owls have become extinct.

It is to be hoped that with a better understanding of the importance of the role of birds of prey in the complex web of life and with active conservation and captive breeding programmes, no more of these birds will be lost, never to return.

ABOUT THIS BOOK

There are some 8600 different bird species distributed around the world, ranging from the tiniest hovering hummingbirds to the great flightless ostrich. Of these, there are almost 300 species of diurnal birds of prey and another 146 species of largely nocturnal owls. Few books, therefore, can hope to be comprehensive not least because the biologies of some of these birds are little known and, in some cases, the birds have only been observed a few times.

Birds of Prey and Owls has been designed to describe and illustrate a small but representative selection of these predatory birds to show their diverse range of sizes, forms, lifestyles, and distribution. It has hardly been possible to include every species of nocturnal or diurnal raptor but, in this one small volume, at least one member of the seven families has been described and, in the case of large and important groups, such as the falcons and the true owls, a sensible selection has been made.

This is not a field guide but, using the fine illustrations and concise but authoritative descriptions in tandem, it should be possible to decide to which family a bird belongs. In addition, if you read through the book, it will give you a good general catalogue of the various types of predatory birds that range the world.

New World Vultures
FAMILY CATHARTIDAE

The New World refers to all the lands which make up the American continents from Tierra del Fuego and the Falkland Islands in the south to Canada in the north. There are seven species of New World vultures: the turkey vulture, the lesser and greater yellow-headed vultures, the American black vulture, the king vulture, and the two species of condor. Like all vultures, they are scavengers feeding mainly on dead and dying animal remains and they perform a vital role in cleaning up the countryside. Although they belong to a different family from the vultures of the Old World, they are similar in form and lifestyle and it may be that they are the more primitive group.

New World vultures are all large birds with huge broad wings that are well adapted for soaring. They lack the powerful killing and grasping feet of the hunting birds of prey and, instead, have feet with short blunt claws and rudimentary hind toes that are better suited to walking and perching. Their bills, although hooked, are small and weak so that they cannot tear open the hides of recently dead animals and are obliged to wait until the corpse decays. Like their Old World cousins, their heads and necks lack feathers so that their plumage does not become fouled as they forage in evil-smelling carcasses. Some species possess tongues which enable them to consume soft, rotted flesh rapidly and they may be able to extract the marrow from broken bones. Although they probably locate their food by sight, they do seem to have a good sense of smell.

They are essentially solitary birds although some species may roost colonially. They nest on cliffs or in hollow trees, and they may use other sites too. Usually, two or three eggs are laid which take about thirty-five days to incubate and the chicks may take as long as three months to fledge.

Turkey Vulture

The turkey vulture is the most widespread of the New World vultures and, in the United States, it is often called a 'turkey buzzard' or 'Johnny crow'. It lives in open country where it is often seen soaring in search of all kinds of carrion and rotting waste. It also feeds along the tideline, on such delicacies as sea lion excrement but, on some Peruvian guano islands, it is a serious predator of the chicks and eggs of other birds. When animals are killed on the roads, turkey vultures are commonly found 'cleaning up' the carcasses.

With their huge, broad wings, essentially all-black plumage, and red, bald heads, they are very distinctive birds although, in flight, they may be confused with other New World vultures. In some places they may be seen gathering in large numbers and, at night, they may roost in flocks of thirty or more birds.

During breeding time, the female usually lays two eggs in a cave or a hollow log on the ground and no real nest is built. Both parents incubate the eggs and care for the young.

It has been thought, wrongly, that turkey vultures carry such diseases of domestic livestock as anthrax and that they are responsible for killing young farm animals in parts of the United States. Therefore, they are often deliberately persecuted, but some also die from feeding upon poisoned carcasses put down to kill coyotes.

Order Falconiformes - diurnal birds of prey (almost 300 species)
Family/Species Cathartidae - New World vultures (7 species)/Turkey Vulture *Cathartes aura*
Length 66-132 cm (26-52 in)

California Condor

The California condor was unknown to science until the end of the eighteenth century. At over 11 kilograms (25 pounds), it is one of the heaviest flying birds in the world and is confined to the mountainous areas of California in the United States. It is exceedingly rare, perhaps numbering less than fifty birds. Although it is a fully protected species, its numbers are still declining through hunting and destruction of its habitat, and it is thought likely to become extinct without further protection and planned breeding programmes. It is not known to prey upon living animals, feeding largely on the carcasses of large animals.

The California condor is an unmistakable bird with its black plumage, bare, orange-red head and neck, and prominent white flashes on its very long, broad wings. Under suitable weather conditions, it is able to soar at great heights in search of carrion and can glide as much as 16 kilometres (10 miles) without so much as a flap of the wings.

The breeding cycle of the California condor is very long. The male displays to the female by facing her, opening and dragging his wings, bowing, and exposing the white wing flashes. After mating, the female lays her single egg on the ground, in a cave, or on a cliff. The young condor is tended and fed by the parent birds for more than a year so that breeding occurs only every other year.

Order Falconiformes - diurnal birds of prey (almost 300 species)

Family/Species Cathartidae - New World vultures (7 species)/California Condor *Gymnogyps californianus*

Length 114-140 cm (45-55 in)

King Vulture

This extraordinary looking bird gets its name from the fact that its large, powerful bill gives it dominance over other scavengers at a carcass. It inhabits the lowland tropical forests and savanna country of the Americas from Mexico to Argentina. From the vantage point of a mountain range, they may be seen soaring in groups over the trees in search of carrion. At this height, their food may be hard to spot and it is thought that they rely heavily on their sense of smell which is better developed than that of most other birds. It has been suggested that they may kill and eat live prey.

In its delicate, creamy adult plumage with black flight feathers, it is easily distinguished from any other New World vulture. The king vulture is a medium-sized bird with broad wings and tail, and its bill and bare neck are bright orange in colour. The bald head is strikingly marked with a blackish-purple crown and its white eyes are ringed in crimson red. The grotesque appearance is lent emphasis by orange wattles and a loosely hanging purple lappet. It is thought that these markings are important in display.

Little is known about the breeding habits of this bird in the wild although, in one instance, a single egg was laid in a hollow tree stump and was incubated by both parents.

Order Falconiformes - diurnal birds of prey (almost 300 species)
Family/Species Cathartidae (7 species)/King Vulture *Sarcorhamphus papa*
Length 79 cm (31 in)

Ospreys
FAMILY PANDIONIDAE

There is only one species included in this family, the
osprey itself. Sometimes, however, it is included within
the family Accipitridae.

Osprey

This migratory, fish-eating bird of prey is found
throughout most of the world inhabiting lakes, rivers,
and coasts. It is the only raptor that feeds almost
exclusively on fish which it catches by plunge-diving
feet first into the water. It grips the fish with its long-
taloned, spike-soled feet and carries it off to a perch,
typically a dead tree, to eat. It particularly likes trout
but any fish will do and it will also prey upon small
mammals and injured birds.

The osprey is dark brown above and snow white
beneath, colours which easily distinguish it from other
medium- or large-sized birds of prey. Its head is
relatively small with a slight crest, and its slit-like
nostrils can be closed when it enters the water. The
wings are long and angled with narrow ends and the
tail is fairly short.

The osprey builds its nest of sticks on the ground,
on islands, or on the tops of trees, adding to the nest
each year so that it becomes extremely large. The hen
lays a clutch of from two to four eggs which she
incubates. During incubation and for the first four
weeks of the fledging period, the male brings food to
the female and to the young.

Order Falconiformes - diurnal birds of prey (almost 300 species)
Family/Species Pandionidae - Osprey (1 species)/ Osprey *Pandion haliaetus*
Length 53-62 cm (21-24 in)

Secretary Birds
FAMILY SAGITTARIIDAE

This family contains only the secretary bird itself. It may not be closely related to any other bird of prey although it resembles a long-legged, ground-living, eagle-like bird.

Secretary Bird

This unique bird is widespread throughout Africa south of the Sahara where it is as typical of the subtropical plains as it is of the tropical savannas. It gets its name from the feathers that sprout from its head, which seem to resemble a bunch of quill pens. Unlike most other birds of prey, the secretary bird is a walker although it can fly quite well. It feeds on almost anything that crawls on the ground from insects to small mammals and birds, and even venomous snakes which it kills by stamping them to death.

The bird is essentially pale grey in colour with black on its wings and with black-feathered thighs. It has long central tail feathers. Its feet bear short, strong toes ideal for walking distances up to 30 kilometres (20 miles) a day but less suitable for grasping prey. Behind its short bill is a patch of bare, red and yellow skin.

Secretary birds pair for life. They are highly territorial at the site of the stick nest built in a tree. The female incubates the two or three eggs for about fifty days.

Order Falconiformes - diurnal birds of prey (almost 300 species)
Family/Species Sagittariidae - secretary birds (1 species)/Secretary Bird *Sagittarius serpentarius*
Length 150 cm (59 in)

Old World Vultures, Hawks, etc

FAMILY ACCIPITRIDAE

This is by far the largest and most varied family of either nocturnal or diurnal birds of prey. In addition to the vultures of the Old World and the true hawks, including the buzzards and eagles, there are kites, honey buzzards, sea eagles, snake eagles, harriers and harrier hawks, chanting goshawks, and so on. The group as a whole ranges every continent of the world except for Antarctica and includes some 218 species. In some older classifications of this family, it was further divided into a number of subfamilies which was convenient and helpful. This arrangement has now been abandoned, largely on the grounds that there is a number of highly specialized, intermediate, or odd forms which could not easily be fitted into any of the subfamilies.

The Old World vultures are similar in form and function to those of the Americas. This is not due to any close relationship but is the result of two distinct families of birds evolving to adapt to similar niches. Thus, these mainly carrion-eating birds are huge and broad winged, and they can remain aloft in search of carcasses for long periods with little effort. It is often possible to see a number of different species of vulture converge on a dead or dying animal but there is a definite pecking order controlling which birds feed first. Male and female vultures tend to be roughly the same size. Vultures are common where carrion is plentiful and rarer in the more affluent parts of Europe and the Middle East. Vultures build huge stick nests in trees or on cliffs and usually lay only one or two eggs.

The remaining 200 or so members of this family vary considerably in size, shape, and way of life but there are some common characteristics. They are long-lived birds with the female being generally larger than the male and sometimes having a differently coloured plumage. Although the wings are generally large and often rounded, they may be broad or narrow, while the tails may be different in shape and length depending upon the habitat and hunting methods. They all have powerful feet with widely spaced toes and sharp talons. There are roughened pads on the soles of their feet which help the birds to grasp their prey. And, of course, they have the typical down-curved bill ideally suited to tearing flesh.

Egyptian Vulture

The Egyptian vulture is a widespread scavenging bird inhabiting all kinds of open country from savannas and mountains to desert edges and beaches, and even towns, throughout southern Europe, Africa, the Middle East, and India. It will often fly long distances in search of food which, in addition to carrion, includes all kinds of organic scraps and rubbish including human excrement. It may gather in large numbers at a carcass but, because of its comparatively small size, it often defers to larger vultures and has to be content with 'tidying up' and picking the bones clean. It is also known to break open the eggs of ostriches, flamingos, and pelicans by picking up the smaller ones and dashing them against a rock or by throwing a stone at the larger eggs.

It is a small, agile vulture with longish legs and a thin, hooked bill. It has long wings and a wedge-shaped tail. It is mainly white in colour with black flight feathers. The face is orange-yellow and the bill is tipped with black. Only the head is bare because it does not feed by inserting its whole head and neck into a bloody carcass.

Following display flights of swoops and dives, both sexes build the stick nest on a sheltered ledge, in a cave in a cliff, or sometimes on a building. Between one and three eggs are laid and both parents incubate them for about forty-two days.

Order Falconiformes - diurnal birds of prey (almost 300 species)

Family/Species Accipitridae - hawks and eagles (about 217 species)/Egyptian Vulture *Neophron percnopterus*

Length 60-70 cm (23.6-27.5 in)

Lammergeier

Also known as the bearded vulture because of the black bristles which extend forwards from its eye region, this uncommon bird mainly inhabits the mountainous areas of southern Europe, Africa, India, and Tibet. It is Europe's rarest vulture. It prefers remote regions although it will also look for food in and around towns and villages. While foraging, it will glide, apparently with little effort, over long distances soaring on the upcurrents along ridges, over forests and steppes, and even through warm valleys and plains. Like the Egyptian vulture, it defers to the larger scavengers at carcasses and is often left only with the bones which it has learned to open by dropping them on to rocks to reveal the marrow; the bird will swallow whole fragments of bone as much as 20 centimetres (8 inches) in length. It may also kill some live animals.

It is a graceful bird with long, narrow wings and a long, wedge-shaped tail. It is brownish-black above with an orange-yellow body and a yellow to near-white head. Its legs are feathered almost to its feet.

Following spectacular display flights over their large breeding territories, lammergeiers build massive nests of branches in a small cave or on an overhung ledge on a cliff, and probably both parents incubate the one or two eggs for about fifty-five days. There may be as many as five alternative nest sites in the territory of one pair.

Order Falconiformes - diurnal birds of prey (almost 300 species)

Family/Species Accipitridae - hawks and eagles (about 217 species)/Lammergeier (Bearded Vulture) *Gypaetus barbatus*

Length 100-115 cm (37-41 in)

Lappet-faced Vulture

With its huge, long, broad wings, massive bulk, powerful hooked bill, and bare head and neck, the lappet-faced vulture is typical of the scavenging Old World vultures. It inhabits the dry, open plains, thornbush savannas, deserts, and mountainous areas of Africa mainly to the east and south of the Sahara, although it does occur in North Africa and an occasional bird has been seen in the south of France. It is Africa's most aggressive vulture and, although it may arrive at a carcass after some of the other scavengers, it frequently drives them away while it feeds. With its powerful, hooked bill, it can even cut through the skin of dead animals. With scarcely a wing beat, it is able to soar and glide long distances in search of carrion.

It is essentially dark brown in colour although, from a distance, it appears black. It has white, feathered thighs and its bare head and neck, ideal for feeding deep inside bloody carcasses, are pinkish to whitish. During the breeding season, from November to March, both sexes build a massive stick nest on the top of a tree or a crag which is added to from year to year. It is probably the female alone that incubates the single egg for a period of about fifty-five days. The young is cared for by both parents.

Order Falconiformes - diurnal birds of prey (almost 300 species)

Family/Species Accipitridae - hawks and eagles (about 217 species)/Lappet-faced Vulture *Torgos tracheliotus*

Length 95-105 cm (37-41 in)

Honey Buzzard

This is mainly a woodland species found throughout most of Europe and into Asia, preferring the mature forests of lowlands and foothills where there are plenty of clearings. It feeds largely on the nests, larvae, and adults of wasps and bees which it locates occasionally from a perch but usually by following the insects on the wing back to their nests. It also feeds on other insects, as well as spiders, amphibians, reptiles, nestling birds, and small mammals. It will take insects in flight but also hunts on the ground. It uses both feet to dig out the nests of bees and wasps. To feed on a live wasp, it skilfully nips off the sting before swallowing it. The honey buzzard is grey-brown above with an ash-grey head contrasting strongly with its yellow eyes. The underparts are almost white with wide barrings and mottlings. The broad wings are also barred. Its feathers are thickly matted to protect it from the stings of bees and wasps.

A breeding pair, which stay together for at least the season, hold a breeding territory and engage in spectacular display flights, with periods of soaring, undulating flights, and wing clapping by the male. Both birds build the nest on the branch of a large tree and it is usually made of twigs with a good deal of greenery. It varies in size and sometimes the birds may make use of an old crow's nest. Both parents incubate the clutch of usually two, purple- or red-spotted white eggs for up to thirty-seven days. Both parents also care for the young. Northern Eurasion honey buzzards migrate to Africa in the Winter.

Order Falconiformes - diurnal birds of prey (almost 300 species)
Family/Species Accipitridae - hawks and eagles (about 217 species)/Honey Buzzard *Pernis apivorus*
Length 52-60 cm (20.4-23.6 in)

Red Kite

Although it is probable that the red kite was once a scavenger of the streets of mediaeval London, it is now confined in Britain to a few Welsh valleys where it breeds in old, open oak woodlands and hunts on the adjacent farmland and rough grazing. It is found throughout much of Europe and into western Asia and North Africa where it circles, soars, and sometimes hovers briefly, often high in the air, in search of carrion and live prey, such as reptiles, birds, and small mammals, which it surprises by dropping out of a steep dive, feet outstretched.

With its long wings, graceful silhouette, and deeply forked, almost transluscent red tail, it is a distinctive bird. The body is mainly a chestnut colour with darker wing tips and trailing edges, while the head is almost white. The undersides of the wings are strongly patterned with black wing tips, and white, rufous, and darker patches. The underside of the tail is pale chestnut with black tips to the forks.

The nest, constructed of dead twigs but lined with softer vegetation, is built by both birds in the fork of a tree, although most of the building materials are brought to the site by the male. Old nests may be used again and added to if the previous season at that nest was successful. Sometimes old buzzard's nests are occupied. One to five, but usually three, eggs are laid and incubated mainly by the female for about thirty-eight days.

Order Falconiformes - diurnal birds of prey (almost 300 species)
Family/Species Accipitridae - hawks and eagles (about 217 species)/Red Kite *Milvus milvus*
Length 60-66 cm (23.6-26 in)

Brahminy Kite

In general, kites, after which the children's toy is named, resemble harriers although they are, in fact, more closely related to fish eagles. The large brahminy kite, particularly, is more akin to the fish eagles in its habits, feeding on frogs, crabs, snakes, fishes, insects, and some carrion. Consequently, it is also known as the white-headed sea eagle. It lives near water and on the coasts of Australasia, southern China, and India where it is sacred in Indian mythology. It also scavenges around human dwellings where it feeds on all kinds of scraps and refuse.

The brahminy kite is reddish brown in colour with distinctive white head and shoulders. Like all kites, it is an excellent flier and can remain virtually stationary in the air for minutes at a time, maintaining its position more by subtle movements of the tail than by using its wings.

The breeding habits of the brahminy kite are reasonably well known. At the breeding site, the birds perform display flights before building the nest which is made of sticks lined with leaves and it is usually situated in a tree or among mangroves. The female lays between one and four eggs (but usually two or three) and incubates them for twenty-six or twenty-seven days while her mate keeps her supplied with food.

Order Falconiformes - diurnal birds of prey (almost 300
   species)
Family/Species Accipitridae - hawks and eagles
   (about 217 species)/Brahminy Kite (White-headed
   Sea Eagle) *Haliastur indus*
Length 46 cm (18 in)

Everglade Kite

Despite the protection it receives from conservation laws, the everglade kite has become extremely rare and is a threatened species in the Florida Everglades from which it gets its name, and in other parts of the southern United States. Throughout the rest of its range in the Caribbean, Mexico, and Central and South America, however, it is quite abundant. The alternative and, perhaps, more appropriate name for this remarkable bird is snail kite for it feeds entirely on a diet of water snails of the genus *Pomacea*.

It is a long-legged bird and, on its long, broad wings, it flaps slowly over the marshy pools where the snails live and, when it sights one, swoops down and picks it up in one foot. Scientists disagree about how the bird then extracts the soft flesh of the snail from its shell but the most likely explanation is that it holds the snail in one foot and then inserts its long, curved, sharply pointed bill into the shell, firstly to remove the protective operculum and then to cut the snail's muscle. The snail can then be easily extracted.

The everglade kite builds a simple nest among marsh grass or in bushes and both parents incubate the clutch of three or four eggs and then care for the young.

Order Falconiformes - diurnal birds of prey (almost 300 species)
Family/Species Accipitridae - hawks and eagles (about 217 species)/Everglade Kite (Snail Kite) *Rostrhamus sociabilis*
Length 38 cm (15 in)

Bald Eagle

The bald eagle is not bald at all but, with its white head plumage contrasting markedly with the overall dark-brown body coloration, it appears, from a distance, to have a bald head. It also has white tail feathers. Although it is the national symbol of the United States of America, is has seriously declined in numbers over the last fifty years and, whereas it was once widespread throughout North America, it is now restricted to isolated pockets, especially along the rivers and lakes of Alaska, where it enjoys rigorous protection. Despite the conservation laws, however, bounties are still paid for their heads.

The bald eagle belongs to a group of mainly fish-eating eagles, most of which are coastal species, and generally called fish or sea eagles. It feeds largely on dead or dying fish, especially on exhausted salmon that have migrated upstream to spawn. It will catch live fishes, however, as well as small mammals.

Following spectacular courtship displays, the birds, which pair for life, build a stick nest in a large tree or on rocks and this is added to from year to year, growing to one of the largest of all birds' nests. The female lays between one and three eggs which mostly she incubates. When the young hatch, the largest and strongest chick is very aggressive and may kill the younger and weaker birds in what is referred to as the 'Cain and Abel battle', so that only one bird survives.

Order Falconiformes - diurnal birds of prey (almost 300 species)
Family/Species Accipitridae - hawks and eagles (about 217 species)/Bald Eagle *Haliaetus leucocephalus*
Length 81-102 cm (32-40 in)

Palm-nut Vulture

The palm-nut vulture is the most atypical of all the vultures both in its appearance and in its feeding habits. Its distribution, in forests, mangroves, and savannas of Africa south of the Sahara, coincides very closely with that of the oil palm on whose fruit it feeds almost exclusively. In the absence of its favourite food, however, it will also eat the fruit of the raphia palm, crabs, molluscs and locusts as well as dead fish in more vulture-like fashion. Because its feeding habits do not require it to delve deeply into the carcasses of dead animals, its neck and head are fully feathered. It is also sometimes called the vulturine fish eagle and it may represent a weak link in a chain of relationships between the Old World vultures and the sea or fish eagles.

The palm-nut vulture does not wander far from its home range and tends to stay near its breeding grounds throughout the year. It builds a stick nest, also using pieces of oil palm, although it may make use of an old nest by repairing it. Only a single egg is laid which is incubated for about forty-four days.

Order Falconiformes - diurnal birds of prey (almost 300
   species)
Family/Species Accipitridae - hawks and eagles
   (about 217 species)/Palm-nut Vulture (Vulturine
   Fish Eagle) *Gypohierax angolensis*
Length 71 cm (28 in)

Bateleur

With its bright livid-red, yellow, and black-tipped bill and black and chestnut-brown-coloured plumage, the bateleur is a magnificent but curious-looking bird. It has exceptionally long, pointed wings and a very short tail so that, in flight, its legs stick out behind and it almost seems to be flying backwards across the sky as it glides long distances, with scarcely a wingbeat, across the plains and savannas of Africa, mainly south of the Sahara, although its range does extend northwards into Iraq.

Although it belongs to a group known as snake eagles or snake hawks, which feed primarily on reptiles, the bateleur eats mainly carrion and it will often aggressively attack other carrion-eating birds to rob them of their meal. It will also kill live prey.

Like its appearance, the bateleur's breeding behaviour is somewhat curious, too, because the adult pairs often seem to tolerate the presence of a juvenile bird near at hand during the whole breeding cycle even though they are not, as a rule, gregarious birds. The birds build a compact, cup-shaped stick nest in a tree and the female lays a single egg which she incubates for about forty-two days. It takes a long time for the young bateleur to fledge and, at first, it is especially weak. During this period it is fed by both parents.

Order Falconiformes - diurnal birds of prey (almost 300 species)
Family/Species Accipitridae - hawks and eagles (about 217 species)/Bateleur (Bateleur Eagle) *Terathopius ecaudatus*
Length 80-85 cm (31.5-33.5 in)

Crested Serpent Eagle

There are some twenty-one subspecies or geographical races of this forest-dwelling bird which vary in size and the tones of the plumage. It is found throughout India to southern China and south-east Asia, including Indonesia and other islands in the region. Like the other snake eagles of the genera *Spilornis* and *Circaetus*, it has short, strong, roughly scaled legs ending in short, strong, rough-surfaced toes which are ideal for subduing and holding the slippery, slithering, and possibly venomous serpents, especially tree snakes, on which it feeds. Although they may be seen soaring above their forest habitat, calling from time to time, they do not hunt from the air, generally preferring to drop down from some vantage point where they perch.

A breeding pair of crested serpent eagles often stay together throughout the year. Following display flights, the pair builds a small, flimsy nest of sticks in a tree. This nest is only used for one year and the next year the pair will build a new nest which may be quite close to that of the previous season or some distance away. Eventually, they may return to the original tree if it is suitable. The female incubates her single egg for about thirty-five days while the male continues to bring her food.

Order Falconiformes - diurnal birds of prey (almost 300 species)

Family/Species Accipitridae - hawks and eagles (about 217 species)/Crested Serpent Eagle *Spilornis cheela*

Length 51-71 cm (20-28 in)

African Harrier Hawk

This is a long-tailed, long-winged, long-legged bird with mainly grey and black plumage and a bare yellow face and dark-tipped bill. In its forest home of tropical Africa south of the Sahara, it is able to feed mainly on small, helpless creatures, such as nestling birds and bats, that no other raptor is able to reach. Its legs are double jointed so that, as it clings with one leg on to the edge of some nook or cranny, such as a hole in a tree, stabilized by its tail, it can insert the other leg into the crevice and bend it as much as 30 degrees backwards to grasp its prey. It will often meticulously and methodically search a dead tree for possible food and will systematically break down the nest of a weaver bird to get at the nestlings.

Unlike the other members of this group of raptors, which nest on the ground, the African harrier hawk nests in a tree. Although the female may lay between one and five eggs, which are incubated by both parents for about forty days, the young have been reported to indulge in a 'Cain and Abel battle' in which the older chick kills the younger ones. The parent birds seem to take no notice of this behaviour.

Order Falconiformes - diurnal birds of prey (almost 300 species)
Family/Species Accipitridae - hawks and eagles (about 217 species)/African Harrier Hawk *Polyboroides typus*
Length 63 cm (25 in)

Hen Harrier

The hen harrier inhabits a wide range of open country, such as steppe, grassland, moors, heaths, the borders of wetlands and even forest clearings or plantations of young trees. It is widely distributed, breeding throughout North America, Europe, and northern to central Asia, migrating southwards to winter when it often roosts communally. It should not be confused with the marsh harrier although, in the United States, it is often referred to as the marsh hawk.

It is a slim, graceful bird with long wings and a long tail. It has long legs ending in small feet which are ideal for grasping its prey of insects and small mammals which it drops on to from its low, searching flight. The male is a mainly bluish-grey bird with white underparts and a white rump and black tips to the wings while the female is a more sombre brown.

The smaller male bird engages in a spectacular plunging and spinning display flight in which he seems to be almost out of control, and at this time, the nest site, on marshy ground or among low vegetation, is chosen. Over a period of about ten days, the female hen harrier lays a clutch of between four and six eggs which she incubates. The male brings food to her and to the chicks after hatching.

Order Falconiformes - diurnal birds of prey (almost 300 species)
Family/Species Accipitridae - hawks and eagles (about 217 species)/Hen Harrier (Marsh Hawk) *Circus cyaneus*
Length 44-52 cm (17-20.5 in)

Dark Chanting Goshawk

The dark chanting goshawk inhabits subtropical and tropical savanna, thick forests and marshes, bush and scrub country with scattered shrubs or trees, and even plantations and orchards. It is found in central and east Africa with small numbers of resident birds in North Africa, Morocco, and the Middle East. The occasional bird has been sighted in Spain.

With its long tail and broad, straight-edged wings, it is a rather bulky looking bird. It is essentially slate grey in colour with white underparts that are finely barred with black. As it perches, sentinel-like, in a tree on its long, orange-red legs waiting to swoop down on some unsuspecting reptile, insect, or small mammal, it is an unmistakable bird. It also catches its food from a rapid stoop or on the ground by running after its prey at a good speed.

Outside the breeding season it is mainly silent, but to attract his mate, the male sings a melodious, chanting call of piping whistles, which is quite distinct from that of any other bird of prey. Both sexes build the flattish, mud-lined, stick nest in a medium-sized, thickly leafed tree and the female lays one or two bluish-white eggs which she incubates; the length of the incubation period is not known.

Order Falconiformes - diurnal birds of prey (almost 300 species)

Family/Species Accipitridae - hawks and eagles (about 217 species)/Dark Chanting Goshawk *Melierax metabates*

Length 38-48 cm (15-19 in)

Goshawk

The goshawk is the largest and most powerful of all the aggressive killers in the genus *Accipiter* and is often trained for falconry. It is exclusively a forest-dwelling bird and prefers spruce and other coniferous woodland. It is widely distributed from North America, through Europe and Asia, to Iran, Tibet, and Japan. The bird is dark greyish-brown above with white barred underparts. The female is similar to the male but much bigger.

With its shortish, rounded wings and long tail, it is well adapted for manoeuvring skilfully among densely packed trees where it usually flies low and fast taking advantage of the cover to swoop upon unsuspecting prey of birds and mammals up to the size of a capercaillie or a hare. It will also attempt to catch birds in flight, stooping from a height like a peregrine. After killing its prey in a vice-like grip from its powerful talons, it usually takes it into cover, plucks it, and eats it on the ground. Except in the breeding season it is usually seen hunting alone.

Goshawks mate for life, the birds reuniting at the beginning of the breeding season and engaging in display flights. Both birds build an untidy stick nest in the fork of a tree or they may reuse an old one. The one to five eggs are incubated mainly by the female for thirty-five to thirty-eight days.

Order Falconiformes - diurnal birds of prey (almost 300
   species)
Family/Species Accipitridae - hawks and eagles
   (about 217 species)/Goshawk *Accipiter gentilis*
Length 48-62 cm (19-24.5 in)

Cooper's Hawk

Cooper's hawk, living in the woodland areas of North America and wintering perhaps as far south as Costa Rica, resembles its cousin the goshawk although it is considerably smaller and its chest is barred with pale brownish orange. It has rounded wings and a long, rounded tail typical of forest-feeding raptors. In addition to preying upon chipmunks and squirrels, this hawk is a bird eater. In the pursuit of such birds as quail, starlings, and blackbirds, it approaches the prey, flapping vigorously and, at the last moment, brakes with spread tail and then throws its feet forwards and upwards, almost turning over, to hit the bird hard from beneath. It also watches for prey from a perch and then swoops down to grasp it and even pursues animals on the ground, partly running and partly flying.

The smaller male defends a territory at the breeding site, feeds the female, and engages in display flights with her. The female lays a clutch of four, five, or even six eggs which she also incubates for the most part. The female Cooper's hawk continues to look after her offspring after incubation, helping them to break out of their shells, and protecting them and feeding them while they are young.

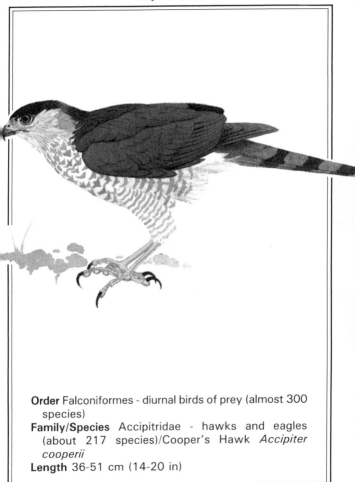

Order Falconiformes - diurnal birds of prey (almost 300 species)
Family/Species Accipitridae - hawks and eagles (about 217 species)/Cooper's Hawk *Accipiter cooperii*
Length 36-51 cm (14-20 in)

Fishing Buzzard

Although, as its name implies, the staple diet of this specialized hawk is fish, it also preys upon lizards, snails, and rodents. It inhabits both forested and open country near water in the tropical lowlands of South America from Mexico to Paraguay and Argentina. Like the osprey, another fish-eating bird of prey, the underparts of its toes are covered with tiny, prickly spines which help it to grasp its slippery quarry. In the more open parts of its range, the bird will swoop down to the water, grasp a fish in its talons and hardly wet its feathers while, elsewhere, it may plunge into the water so that it is obliged to dry its plumage afterwards.

It is distinctively marked with a brownish body, dark tail and wing tips, a pale head, and a dark bill. On the lighter-coloured throat there is a dark band. The fishing buzzard has long, broad wings, a short, broad tail, and a hooked bill.

Little, not even the number of eggs laid, is known about the breeding behaviour of this bird.

Order Falconiformes - diurnal birds of prey (almost 300 species)

Family/Species Accipitridae - hawks and eagles (about 217 species)/Fishing Buzzard *Busarellus nigricollis*

Length 46-51 cm (18-20 in)

Buzzard

With the exception of the kestrel, the buzzard is the commonest and perhaps best known bird of prey in Europe. It is a bird of woodlands, moorlands, and open country, including cultivated areas, and is found throughout the whole of Europe across central Asia to the Far East as far as Japan. It also winters in Asia Minor, East Africa, Malaysia, and southern China. It is a medium-sized compact bird with fairly broad, rounded wings and a short tail. Its colour varies considerably but most commonly it is a dark to medium-brown bird with a greyish or brownish head. Its underparts may be brown with a paler crescent on the breast or vice versa. From below, the wing tips and trailing edges are conspicuously darker. The tail may be barred.

The buzzard feeds on a wide variety of animals in a number of ways and is not averse to scavenging from carrion. It preys upon small mammals, birds, reptiles, amphibians, insects, and even earthworms. It may pounce on its quarry from a perch, soar and hover over open ground before dropping from the sky and making the final kill on the ground, or even take insects when standing or walking.

After uncharacteristically energetic courtship flights, both birds build a substantial stick nest on a tree, rocky crag, cliff, or even on sloping ground. The female lays two to five or, rarely, six eggs which are incubated by both birds for thirty-three to thirty-eight days.

Order Falconiformes - diurnal birds of prey (almost 300 species)
Family/Species Accipitridae - hawks and eagles (about 217 species)/Buzzard *Buteo buteo*
Length 51-56 cm (20-22 in)

Red-tailed Hawk

In North America, the birds of the genus *Buteo* are referred to as hawks rather than buzzards, and the red-tailed hawk resembles the common buzzard of Eurasia although it is larger, thicker set, and has a conspicuous rusty or chestnut-coloured tail as do some birds from the eastern populations of its cousin. It is an aggressive hawk with a loud voice and it swoops down on its prey of rodents, rabbits, snakes, lizards, birds, such as pheasants, and insects either from a perch or from flight. It inhabits woodland, open heath and moorland, grassland, mountainous areas, or the open desert, in North and Central America and the West Indies.

Following display flights over the breeding territory, a nest of sticks is built in a tree or on a cactus and the female remains there for some weeks before laying between one and four eggs. She is fed by the male throughout this period and both birds incubate the eggs for twenty-eight to thirty-two days.

Order Falconiformes - diurnal birds of prey (almost 300 species)
Family/Species Accipitridae - hawks and eagles (about 217 species)/Red-tailed Hawk *Buteo jamaicensis*
Length 46-61 cm (18-24 in)

Harpy Eagle

The harpy eagle is one of the world's largest flying birds and is certainly the most formidable. It is found only among the dense growth of tropical forest from southern Mexico to eastern Bolivia and northern Argentina where, for such a huge bird, it flies on its short wings with remarkable agility using its long tail to steer. Sadly, this magnificent bird is becoming rarer as its habitat has been relentlessly destroyed and many birds have been shot by hunters for their feathers. It is basically a black-and-white bird with a white facial disc and two black tufts on its crown which can be erected, possibly in threat display.

As it flies from tree to tree beneath the forest canopy, it is ever watchful for a possible meal of tree-living mammals, such as monkeys, lemurs, or sloths, which it chases, grabs, and then kills using its huge feet armed with wickedly pointed talons.

Its breeding behaviour is not very well known, as the bird builds a stick nest or platform high in the tops of the tallest trees and observations are difficult. Possibly two eggs are laid and the young birds may stay with their parents for a long time, perhaps to ensure that the eaglets become stronger and are better able to survive the period between fledging and maturity. It is probable that, if young are successfully reared in one season, breeding occurs only in alternate years.

Order Falconiformes - diurnal birds of prey (almost 300 species)
Family/Species Accipitridae - hawks and eagles (about 217 species)/Harpy Eagle *Harpia harpyja*
Length 90 cm (35.5 in)

Golden Eagle

As the golden eagle swoops into its eyrie, high on a cliff ledge, the grouse carried in its powerful talons seems dwarfed by such a magnificent predator. Although it is still one of the world's most numerous large eagles, ranging from Britain right through Europe and Asia to North America and even into North Africa, it has now been driven by human intervention and persecution into the hills and mountains.

It is a complete master of the air rising, apparently without effort, on thermal updrafts only to soar with scarcely a wingbeat and at surprising speeds across the hills and valleys for long distances in search of its prey which it dives down upon and kills on the ground. It has been said to take large numbers of lambs and, although it may kill some, it seems likely that it preys only on weak or sickly specimens. It is a great brown bird, with a wingspan of as much as 2.2 metres (more than 7 feet), and only the adult birds bear the golden head which gives the species its name.

After the spectacular display flights over the nest site (there may be several nests, or eyries), the female usually lays two eggs which she incubates for forty-three to forty-five days. The stronger and older of the two chicks often kills the younger weaker bird in a 'Cain and Abel battle'.

Order Falconiformes - diurnal birds of prey (almost 300 species)
Family/Species Accipitridae - hawks and eagles (about 217 species)/Golden Eagle *Aquila chrysaetos*
Length 76-89 cm (30-35 in)

Falcons
FAMILY FALCONIDAE

This family of some sixty species of diurnal birds of prey includes the true falcons, falconets, and pygmy falcons, the caracaras and milvagos, the laughing falcons, and the forest falcons.

The true falcons, such as the peregrine, have long, pointed wings and are mainly powerful hunters of birds and other prey which they catch on the wing and their legs are thickened and strengthened to withstand the tremendous impact as they strike. The ugly-looking caracaras and milvagos are carrion eaters or feed on wasps rather like the unrelated honey buzzard. Unlike the typical falcons, these birds build their own nests and occur only in the central and southern Americas. The snake-eating laughing falcon and the forest falcons also live in this part of the world, resembling and behaving more like the hawks of the Accipitridae with their long tails and relatively short, rounded wings and legs.

The falcons are found throughout the world and although only a few of them build nests for themselves, they all lay eggs which are reddish-buff coloured on the inside of the shell. Like the accipiters, they have typical, flesh-tearing, hooked bills and powerful, curved talons on their feet. Although the males and females may resemble one another, the female is usually the larger bird. All of the true falcons, as well as the caracaras, have two teeth-like cutting serrations on the upper mandible of the bill with two corresponding notches in the lower part. The falcons use these 'teeth' for breaking the neck of their prey after they have caught them with their feet.

Common Caracara

The common caracara belongs to a small group of birds which, although they are classified as falcons, seem more like a cross between vultures and crows. In its various subspecies, this bird occupies open country from as far south as the Falkland Islands to the southern United States, even breeding in central Florida. With its bare face, it resembles a long-legged vulture and, indeed, like vultures, it feeds by scavenging on all kinds of carrion and plant material, as well as on worms, beetles and other insects, lizards, fish, and small mammals which it catches by searching on foot. Caracaras also scavenge in towns and along roadsides where carrion is plentiful and it has been said that they will follow cars and trains in anticipation of scraps.

Little is known about the breeding behaviour of most species of caracara. It seems, however, that, unlike many other members of this family, the common caracara builds its own flimsy stick nest usually in a tree or on the ground. The female lays a clutch of two to four eggs which are incubated by both parents for about twenty-eight days. The young, which stay in the nest for between two and three months, are fed and cared for by both birds.

Order Falconiformes - diurnal birds of prey (almost 300 species)
Family/Species Falconidae - falcons (60 species)/ Common Caracara *Polyborus plancus*
Length 56-61 cm (22-24 in)

Barred Forest Falcon

The barred forest falcon is a strange and little-known bird, inhabiting the undergrowth of the densest forests from southern Mexico to northern Argentina. It is well adapted to its predatory life in the impenetrable jungles, having short wings and long tail and legs. It is able to manoeuvre efficiently among the trees and waits in cover to attack its prey of birds, small mammals, such as mice, and lizards. It specializes in following soldier ants and then attacks the birds that normally feed upon them.

Largely because the barred forest falcon is so difficult to observe, virtually nothing is known about its breeding behaviour, but it seems likely that it lays its eggs in a hollow tree stump like the snake-eating laughing falcon (*Herpetotheres cachinnans*) from the same part of the world.

Order Falconiformes - diurnal birds of prey (almost 300
  species)
Family/Species Falconidae - falcons (60 species)/
  Barred Forest Falcon *Micrastur ruficollis*
Length 33-38 cm (13-15 in)

Collared Falconet

The collared falconet is one of five species belonging to the genus *Microhierax*, the smallest birds of prey in the world. Behaving more like a flycatcher than a true raptor, it flies above the trees in its forest home on the hills and lowlands of Asia from the Himalayas and northern India to south-east Asia, where it catches aerial insects and some small birds on the wing.

Not much is known about its breeding behaviour but it seems that it lays its four or five eggs in the disused hole nest of a woodpecker or a barbet. Unlike the eggs of the cliff-ledge laying falcons, which are coloured a concealing red-brown, those of this tiny falconet are white perhaps because they have lost the need to be camouflaged.

Order Falconiformes - diurnal birds of prey (almost 300 species)
Family/Species Falconidae - falcons (60 species)/ Collared Falconet (Red-legged Falconet) *Microhierax caerulescens*
Length 19 cm (7.5 in)

Common Kestrel

The various species of kestrels are probably among the most familiar falcons throughout the world and the Common Kestrel of Europe, Asia, and Africa is no exception. In Britain this bird is often colloquially known as the windhover, because of its habit of hovering, virtually stationary, holding its position with rapid wingbeats and subtle movements of the tail. It inhabits all kinds of open country and cultivated land and has now adapted to urban life. The common kestrel is frequently seen hovering some 10 to 15 metres (30 to 50 feet) above motorway verges searching, with its keen eyesight, for its prey of small mammals or insects which it gently drops down upon. Various suggestions have been put forward to explain this behaviour but it seems likely that motorways represent barriers to small animals on the move so that they congregate in larger numbers at their edges. The kestrel also catches birds and other animals by direct attack and almost always eats its food on the ground or takes it away to a perch.

With its warm brown coloration, long wings and tail, and singular hunting habits, it is unlikely to be mistaken for any other bird except, perhaps the lesser kestrel.

It lays its large clutch of four to nine eggs on a ledge, in a hole or fork of a tree, on buildings, or in nest boxes. The eggs are usually incubated by the female for twenty-seven to twenty-nine days.

Order Falconiformes - diurnal birds of prey (almost 300
  species)
Family/Species Falconidae - falcons (60 species)/
  Common Kestrel *Falco tinnunculus*
Length 32-35 cm (12.5-14 in)

Hobby

In flight, this slightly built, elegant, long-winged, and relatively short-tailed falcon resembles a large swift. It has dark grey upper parts with a paler, streaked underbody and characteristic rufous thighs and undertail. It also has a conspicuous white collar and dark moustachial streaks. It is found flying over all kinds of open country, bush and savanna, from Britain to China, and it winters in southern Africa and the Far East.

It is a remarkably fast and manoeuvrable flier, and is even able to catch birds such as swallows on the wing. It feeds mainly on flying birds, insects, and sometimes bats which it catches with its feet from a downward or upward stoop or even by pursuit in level flight. It will also seize the opportunity of capturing small mammals on the ground, diving down from a perch or from searching or hovering flight. The hobby even steals the food that has been caught by kestrels.

The hobby does not build its own nest, but the female lays her two to four eggs in the abandoned nest of another bird, especially that of a crow. The lining may be removed from the nest and the same one may be reused year after year. Incubation, for twenty-eight to thirty-one days, is mainly carried out by the female, although the male feeds her during this period and also brings food to the nest when the chicks have hatched.

Order Falconiformes - diurnal birds of prey (almost 300
   species)
Family/Species Falconidae - falcons (60 species)/
   Hobby *Falco subbuteo*
Length 30-36 cm (12-14 in)

Brown Hawk

Despite its usual name, which it gets from its appearance and behaviour, especially its feeding methods, this bird is a true falcon and is also called the brown falcon. It is one of the commonest birds of prey in the open country of Australia and is also found in New Guinea, Tasmania, and Dampier Island. Typically it is a nomadic bird.

Like the other falcons, it is quite capable of rapid flight, but generally it is less active than other members of the genus preferring to spend a good deal of its time on a perch. It preys upon mammals, such as rabbits, young birds, reptiles, and insects, which it kills on the ground. The brown hawk also feeds upon some carrion.

Its breeding behaviour is reasonably well known and, like most other falcons, the female brown hawk usually lays her clutch of two to four eggs in the abandoned nest of another bird, although it may also actively build its own stick nest. Both parents are involved in the incubation.

Order Falconiformes - diurnal birds of prey (almost 300
  species)
Family/Species Falconidae - falcons (60 species)/
  Brown Hawk (Brown Falcon) *Falco berigora*
Length 40-51 cm (16-20 in)

Gyrfalcon

The gyrfalcon is the largest, most powerful, and most impressive of all the true falcons and is much in demand by falconers, able as it is to knock a bird as big as a heron out of the sky. The bird has long, broad-based, and rather round-tipped wings and a long tail, and varies considerably in colour from an almost uniform dark grey to virtually pure white. In the northern tundra gyrfalcons feed almost exclusively on ptarmigan, and the breeding success of this falcon seems to be directly linked to the abundance of its prey.

Though its numbers are declining everywhere through persecution and the attention of egg collectors, the gyrfalcon is found throughout northern, mainly arctic Europe, Asia, and North America where it finds disused nests on overhanging cliffs, mountains, river crags, or occasionally trees, and hunts low to the ground mainly over open country with sparse plant cover.

The three to four eggs are incubated for thirty-four to thirty-six days mostly by the female although the male will sit while she is away feeding. Initially, the female cares for and feeds the young with food brought by the male but later both birds hunt for and feed the chicks.

Order Falconiformes - diurnal birds of prey (almost 300
   species)
Family/Species Falconidae - falcons (60 species)/
   Gyrfalcon *Falco rusticolus*
Length 50-60 cm (20-24 in)

Peregrine

The peregrine falcon is distributed throughout most of the world and often lives in mountainous country or around sea cliffs. During the winter it may be found on estuaries. It feeds mainly on birds and hunts on the wing making a dramatic, high-speed dive, or stoop, at its prey, killing it instantly in an explosion of feathers with a blow of its powerful talons. Sometimes, it may chase its victim through the air, and it can manoeuvre with supreme ease. With the gyrfalcon, it is highly valued for the sport of falconry.

The seventeen different races of the peregrine vary considerably in colour but, essentially, it is dark grey above and finely barred beneath with dark moustachial stripes. It has yellow legs, a yellow, black-tipped bill, and yellow rings around the eyes. It is a robust bird with tapered, pointed wings and a short, slim tail so that, when seen in flight, it appears anchor shaped. Like other birds of prey, peregrines are often mobbed by small birds but will themselves mob other raptors, such as eagles.

Following spectacular flight displays, the peregrine begins breeding in April, laying its two to six eggs on a cliff ledge, a building, or on the ground. The female does most of the incubation and is fed by the male.

Order Falconiformes - diurnal birds of prey (almost 300
  species)
Family/Species Falconidae - falcons (60 species)/
  Peregrine *Falco peregrinus*
Length 38-51 cm (15-20 in)

Barn Owls, Grass Owls, and Bay Owls

FAMILY TYTONIDAE

There are only twelve species comprising this family and they differ from true owls, the Strigidae, in a number of small ways, such as in plumage and skeletal details. Their chief feature is the possession of a heart-shaped facial disc, although this is less well developed in the bay owls. The second and third toes of barn owls are the same length whereas in the true owls, the second toe is shorter, and the middle toe of barn owls has a comb-like edge to the claw. The breastbone and wishbone of the members of this family are joined, while among the Strigidae they are separated. Like most birds of prey, however, barn owls have powerful toes with sharp, curved talons and a hooked bill although this is almost concealed by feathers.

The facial discs surround relatively small eyes but it is thought that the discs are involved in the detection of sound rather than with vision. It is not known precisely how they work but they do seem to help in directing even the tiniest single sound into the large, asymmetrically positioned ears just behind them. And it is in the particularly nocturnal species, such as the barn owl, in which these structures are best developed. By turning and bobbing their heads and with the aid of mobile ear flaps, it seems that a barn owl can precisely locate the position of a small prey animal in total darkness from just one sound.

The ghostly white barn owl with its forward-facing

eyes and beautiful, white facial disc is associated with
'things that go bump in the night' throughout much of
the world. Indeed, barn owls may even have been
responsible for some of the unsubstantiated reports of
unidentified flying objects, or UFOs. On dark nights at
certain times of the year, their underparts literally seem
to glow in the dark, perhaps as a result of the
accumulation of phosphorescent algae on their plumage.
As they quarter the ground in search of prey, in the
darkness where size is difficult to estimate, UFO-
watchers might be forgiven for thinking that they are
looking at some well-lit alien spacecraft, particularly
when the bioluminescence suddenly 'switches off'!

The ears and eyes of these owls occupy a good deal
of the skull cavity so there is little room for a brain. Thus,
the idea of the 'wise old owl' must stem more from their
vaguely human appearance rather than from any real
intelligence.

Bay Owl

There are only two known species of bay owls of which the African species, the Tanzanian bay owl, has only recently been discovered. They are grouped with the barn owls on the grounds of certain similarities of body form and structure. Like the barn owl, the bay owl, also known as the oriental bay owl, has long, feathered legs and the characteristic facial disc, although the latter is less geometrically shaped and the face of the bird is less appealing to the human observer.

Little is known about the life histories of these curious night hunters which live in the forests of northern India, south-east Asia, and Sri Lanka. It is generally thought that they feed on insects which they hunt in and around the trees.

They probably lay between three and five eggs in a hole in a tree.

Order Strigiformes - owls (146 species)
Family/Species Tytonidae - barn owls, grass owls, and
   bay owls (12 species)/Bay Owl (Oriental Bay Owl)
   Phodilus badius
Length 29 cm (11.5 in)

Barn Owl

The barn owl is found throughout the world except for temperate Asia and many Pacific islands. It was originally a bird of rocky country, but now lives in more open habitats, woodlands, and inhabited areas where it patrols over fields and heaths during the dying evening light to catch its prey of small rodents and birds which it kills on the ground.

The upper parts of the bird are coloured a pale, rufous yellow with a greyish mottling. The underside can occur in two main colour phases, ranging from rufous brown to pure white with some darker specks, and the facial disc is always the same colour as the breast. It is a fairly long-legged bird and the legs, which resemble the letter X when the bird is perching, are feathered down to the claws.

Barn owls generally live alone or in pairs and roost during the day in farm buildings or in holes in trees. In some parts of its range, its numbers have declined dramatically through reduction of its nesting sites as the barns have been modernized, and through the use of pesticides.

Breeding usually begins in April in the north. The female nests in an old building, a hollow tree trunk, or a rock crevice, and lays four to seven eggs which she incubates for about thirty-three days. The male brings her food and both parents care for the young.

Order Strigiformes - owls (146 species)
Family/Species Tytonidae - barn owls, grass owls, and
  bay owls (12 species)/Barn Owl *Tyto alba*
Length 34 cm (13.5 in)

True Owls
FAMILY STRIGIDAE

Although the wood owls of the genus *Strix*, with their feathered feet and rounded wings, do have well-developed facial discs like the barn owls, most of the genera in this large family do not. They all tend to have large, forward-facing eyes and most have reduced or flattened facial discs which make them look as though they are frowning. There are 134 species in this family and they are to be found throughout the world except in Antarctica and some oceanic islands, except where they have been introduced by humans to control pests, such as rats.

There are far fewer species of the night-hunting owls than there are of the diurnal raptors and they are less diverse in form and mode of life. All owls look like owls whereas not everyone would think that the secretary bird, for example, belonged to the same order as, say, a kestrel. The true owls range in size from the tiny least pygmy owl at a mere 12 centimetres (4.5-5 inches) to the eagle owl at 68 centimetres (27 inches). Typically, owls of this family are soft-feathered, short-tailed birds with the typical down-curved bill, usually partly concealed by feathers. They are coloured to blend with their various backgrounds so, while most are various shades of mottled brown, those living in the northern coniferous forests are usually greyer in colour, while the snowy owl, which spends a good deal of time on snow-covered ground, varies from pure white to white speckled and barred with black.

Unlike many of the eagles, hawks, and falcons, most owls spend a lot of time searching for prey from a perch and then drop from there silently on to it. The prey animals, which include insects, fishes, birds, and mammals, are usually swallowed whole and the indigestible parts, such as feathers and bones, are regurgitated as a compact pellet. Not all owls hunt at night and the fishing owls, for example, scoop fish from the water during the day using their spiny feet. Most true owls are hole nesters although some, such as the snowy owl, nest on the ground. They usually lay white eggs because there is little need for them to be camouflaged.

Brown Fish Owl

The brown fish owl is one of seven species of semi-aquatic, fish-eating owls. They are all big, powerful, day-flying birds which scoop fishes from the surface of the water in their strong feet which are covered with prickles to help them grip their slippery prey. The feet and ankles of the brown fish owl are not feathered so that the bird is able to wade into shallow water in search of prey without wetting its plumage. It is always found in or around forested lakes and streams in an area from the Middle East to southern China including south-east Asia and Sri Lanka.

The facial disc of this bird is considerably reduced, but it does have conspicuous ear tufts. Its wings are short, as is typical of forest-dwelling predatory birds, and it is able to fly in and out among the trees with considerable agility.

The brown fish owl makes a nest platform in a tree by joining some branches together or it may nest on a ledge or rock. The female lays one or two eggs which are incubated by both parents for about thirty-five days.

Order Strigiformes - owls (146 species)
Family/Species Strigidae - true owls (134 species)/
Brown Fish Owl *Ketupa zeylonensis*
Length 56 cm (22 in)

Elf Owl

At only about the size of a sparrow, the elf owl is probably the world's smallest owl. It inhabits wooded canyons, pinewoods, desert with saguaro cactus, and even gardens, in the south-western United States from southern Texas to south-eastern California and Mexico. It is a buff-coloured, short-tailed bird with yellow eyes and no ear tufts. Interestingly, if it is captured, it pretends to be dead until it is released or it is certain that any danger has passed.

It emerges at dusk from its daytime roost in a tree to feed almost exclusively on insects which it may capture in flight with its feet or it may dart out from a perch rather like a flycatcher. It will also occasionally take mice, snakes, lizards, and even scorpions, having either removed or crushed the sting before swallowing .

After the male bird has found a suitable nesting site in a deserted woodpecker hole in a cactus or tree trunk, he sings to attract the female which enters the nest to lay her clutch of one to five (usually three) white eggs. She incubates the eggs for about twenty-four days while the male feeds her. He continues to bring food to the nest in which the female feeds the young after they have hatched.

Order Strigiformes - owls (146 species)
Family/Species Strigidae - true owls (134 species)/
Elf Owl *Micrathene whitneyi*
Length 14 cm (5.5 in)

Screech Owl

The screech owl inhabits open woodland, cactus desert, old orchards, and suburban areas, from Mexico in the south to the tree line of North America and Canada. Despite its name, its most usual calls include soft purrs and a descending wail. It is a small owl with conspicuous ear tufts and yellow eyes. The mottled plumage exists in two colour phases of rufous or grey. During the day, it roosts in a hollow tree or old building, emerging at dusk to feed on insects, small mammals, amphibians, reptiles, and some birds. Given the opportunity, however, it will eat almost any living animal.

The birds lay their three to eight white eggs in an unlined tree cavity, such as a disused woodpecker hole, or even in a nest box. They defend their nest sites aggressively and any unsuspecting person passing too close to the spot at night is liable to be struck on the head. The eggs are incubated by the female while the male brings her food and, after the eggs have hatched, both birds feed and care for the chicks.

Order Strigiformes - owls (146 species)
Family/Species Strigidae - true owls (134 species)/
  Screech Owl *Otus asio*
Length 18-25 cm (7-10 in)

Snowy Owl

The beautiful great white snowy owl inhabits all kinds of open country, from tundra and marshes to dunes and plains, around the northern polar areas of arctic Canada, Greenland, Britain, Europe, and Asia. In colour, it ranges from pure white to white with dark spotting, to blend with its background which is often snow covered. The female is usually darker and larger than the male. It has a round head with yellow eyes, broad, rounded wings, and its feet are feathered to its talons. Except during the breeding season, when it emits hoarse croaks and shrill whistles, it is silent and solitary.

It is a day-hunting owl, usually flying low and fast over the ground in search of mammals, such as arctic hares and lemmings, smaller rodents, birds, such as gulls and ducks, and even dead fish on beaches or rats at Norwegian rubbish dumps.

At breeding time, it makes a shallow scrape in the ground or on a rock on open tundra, which it lines with feathers, moss, and lichens. It usually lays between five and eight white eggs, although as many as fifteen have been recorded in seasons when food is abundant. The female incubates the eggs for about thirty-two days while the male keeps her supplied with food.

Snowy Owl

Order Strigiformes - owls (146 species)
Family/Species Strigidae - true owls (134 species)/
  Snowy Owl *Nyctea scandiaca*
Length 52-65 cm (20.5-25.5 in)

Great Horned Owl

The great horned owl is the biggest and most powerful of the American so-called 'eared' owls although this name refers to prominent tufts on top of the head which are merely feathers and not ears at all. It is found in a wide variety of habitats from woods and forests to deserts, swamps, open country, and even city parks and suburbs. It is found throughout the Americas from Tierra del Fuego to Alaska. It is catholic in its choice of food, taking mammals as large as cats, as well as birds, such as grouse, reptiles, amphibians, and insects. Usually roosting in trees during the day, it hunts mainly at night although in remote, unpopulated areas, it will also feed in daylight. The great horned owl has yellowish eyes and its plumage ranges in colour from mottled grey and dark brown to almost white with a white throat conspicuous in the darker birds.

In parts of its range this owl can be one of the first birds to nest, as early as January or February when there is still snow on the ground. It usually lays two or three, but sometimes as many as six, white eggs on the bare surface of a cliff ledge, a cave, or a hollow in a tree but it will also make use of the abandoned nest of another bird. Both parents incubate the eggs for thirty to thirty-five days and are very aggressive in the defence of the young.

Order Strigiformes - owls (146 species)
Family/Species Strigidae - true owls (134 species)/
   Great Horned Owl *Bubo virginianus*
Length 46-64 cm (18-25 in)

Boobook Owl

The boobook or morepork owl is a smallish owl which ranges throughout wooded, scrub, and open areas of Australasia, and gains its odd name from the aboriginal word to describe its call. In certain parts of New Zealand, it is suffering as a result of fierce competition with another small but aggressive species, the little owl, which was introduced there little more than sixty years ago. Although it occasionally hunts during the day, this owl usually roosts in caves and starts to seek its prey of insects, especially moths, spiders, reptiles, small birds, and mammals at dusk. Small prey is usually carried in the bird's bill.

The boobook owl builds its nest in a hollow tree, a cavity left in a broken tree, or sometimes in a patch of thick undergrowth. The female usually lays her clutch of three or four eggs at two-day intervals and incubates them for thirty to thirty-one days beginning from the laying of the first egg. The young owls are cared for in the nest by both parents for about thirty-five days.

Order Strigiformes - owls (146 species)
Family/Species Strigidae - true owls (134 species)/
Boobook Owl (Morepork Owl) *Ninox novaeseelandiae*
Length 29 cm (11.4 cm)

Long-eared Owl

The long-eared owl is a mottled-brown bird about the size of a crow with long wings, long, closely spaced ear tufts, and pale, chestnut-coloured facial discs. It is one of the most nocturnal of all owls and, except during the breeding season when it produces a variety of whistles, hoots, and other calls, it is essentially silent. During the day, it roosts in a tree, aligning itself along the trunk so that it is very difficult to see although its presence may be detected by the piles of pellets (regurgitated bones, feathers, and so on) that accumulate beneath the roost. It is found in woodlands throughout Europe, Asia, north-west Africa, and North America but it does hunt in open country. It is an adaptable bird and feeds on a variety of small mammals, such as mice and bats, as well as on some birds and insects.

Long-eared owls prefer to lay their usually four to five white eggs in the nest of a crow, hawk, or squirrel, although in some parts of their range, such as on the Shetland Isles, they may nest on the ground. The eggs are incubated by the female for twenty-six to twenty-eight days while the male brings her food. After hatching, the young stay in the nest for three or four weeks and, if intruders approach, the parents will engage in a spectacular threat display.

Order Strigiformes - owls (146 species)
Family/Species Strigidae - true owls (134 species)/
   Long-eared Owl *Asio otus*
Length 33-49 cm (13-16 in)

Hawk Owl

As its name suggests, the hawk owl behaves more like a hawk than an owl, hunting during the day for rodents and other small mammals, as well as birds and insects. It inhabits the clearings in coniferous woodlands or the fields which border them, throughout Canada and the extreme northern United States as well as northern Europe and northern Asia. It searches for its prey from an exposed perch, such as the branch of a tree, and then swoops down upon it; the hawk owl may also hover like a kestrel and it has a fast, hawk-like flight. It is a distinctive-looking owl with yellow eyes, a barred breast, pale facial discs edged with black, relatively short, pointed wings, and an unusually long tail.

Depending upon the availability of food, the female lays between three and nine, but usually five or six, white eggs in a tree cavity, the abandoned nest of another bird, a woodpecker hole, or, rarely, on a cliff. The eggs are incubated mainly by the female for twenty-five to thirty days and, because of intervals between laying the eggs, there is a marked difference in the size of the young.

Order Strigiformes - owls (146 species)
Family/Species Strigidae - true owls (134 species)/
   Hawk Owl *Surnia ulula*
Length 38-43 cm (15-17 in)

Pygmy Owl

This is the smallest European owl and it inhabits open areas in mixed or coniferous forests of northern Europe through to Russia, central Asia, and China. Its upper parts are dark brown, spotted with white and its underside is greyish white with barrings and mottlings. Its tail is unusually long for such a small bird and the facial discs on its small head are not very apparent because of the patterning of the feathers in dark, concentric circles. Many of the other species of pygmy owls often fly and hunt during the day but this bird is largely nocturnal feeding on small rodents and birds which may be caught in flight. When food is plentiful, it may store it in tree cavities. Despite its small size, it is an efficient hunter and may even kill animals larger than itself.

During autumn evenings and early mornings, the pygmy owl flies among the branches of its woodland home singing its melodious song of soft whistles ending in a trill.

It lays its two to eight eggs in a tree cavity or in the disused hole of a woodpecker. The eggs are incubated by the female for about twenty-eight days while the male brings her food.

Order Strigiformes - owls (146 species)
Family/Species Strigidae - true owls (134 species)/
  Pygmy Owl *Glaucidium passerinum*
Length 16 cm (6 in)

Little Owl

Although it is larger than the pygmy owl, the little owl is still a small bird with a flat-topped head, low and prominent 'eyebrows', and large yellow eyes giving it a stern, almost frowning expression. It has brown upper parts, spotted with white, while the paler under side has darker markings. It inhabits all kinds of open country with scattered trees and bushes, throughout most of Europe, west and central Asia, to northern Africa. It has been introduced to Britain and New Zealand. It is quite common around villages and in parks, gardens, and cemeteries but it avoids dense woodland.

During the day, the little owl roosts in trees or hollows in walls and emerges at dusk to feed on insects, such as moths, small rodents, birds, and even carrion. Other birds may mob it at its roost site and drive it off. It makes a variety of sounds from a flute-like call note to dog-like barkings and other strange cries.

It makes use of a variety of nest sites including tree holes, ledges on rocks or buildings, abandoned burrows, and the old nest of another bird. The female incubates the three to five eggs for about twenty-nine days while the male brings food to her and to the newly hatched chicks.

Order Strigiformes - owls (146 species)
Family/Species Strigidae - true owls (134 species)/
  Little Owl *Athene noctua*
Length 21 cm (8.25 in)

Tawny Owl

The tawny owl is strongly built with a large rounded head, broad rounded wings, and characteristic dark, almost black eyes. It has no ear tufts. Its upper parts are usually a mottled reddish-brown, tawny, or occasionally grey colour while the underside is paler with dark streaks. It inhabits woods, gardens, parks, and urban areas throughout Britain, Europe, North Africa, and west and central Asia. It is Europe's most common and widespread owl and although it occasionally hunts during the day, it is essentially nocturnal and its well-known hooting calls are heard more often than the bird is seen. During the day, it roosts in a tree and, if spotted, will be mobbed by other birds. It feeds on a wide range of small mammals, birds, reptiles, amphibians, fishes, and insects.

It uses all kinds of nest sites from chimneys, tree holes, rabbit holes, and magpie nests to rocks and the bare ground. Usually two to five eggs are laid and incubated by the female for twenty-eight to thirty days. Initially, the male brings food to the nest for the newly hatched young but later both parents hunt.

Order Strigiformes - owls (146 species)
Family/Species Strigidae - true owls (134 species)/
  Tawny Owl *Strix aluco*
Length 36-40 cm (14-16 in)

Burrowing Owl

The unique and rather comical burrowing owl resembles a long-legged little owl. It has basically brownish-grey mottled plumage, a short tail, no ear tufts, yellow eyes, and a white face. Unusually, the male is slightly bigger than the female. It lives largely on the ground in the open plains, semideserts, deserts, fields, and even airports of the Americas from south-west Canada right down the western United States to Tierra del Fuego.

Burrowing owls feed on a variety of prey, including insects, small mammals, birds, reptiles, and amphibians, which they often hunt on the ground. They have frequently been noticed following large moving animals, such as dogs or horses, perhaps to catch the small animals that are disturbed. Both adults and young may be seen during the day at the entrances to their nest burrows although they generally hunt in the evening. When disturbed, burrowing owls make good use of their long legs by running to cover.

Burrowing owls usually make use of the burrows of animals, such as prairie dogs, but they may also use their feet to scrape out their own nest burrow as well as to enlarge the nesting chamber in an abandoned hole; the chamber may be lined with dried animal faeces. They are known to live in loose breeding colonies. The female lays between six and eleven eggs which are incubated for about twenty-eight days by both parents.

Order Strigiformes - owls (146 species)
Family/Species Strigidae - true owls (134 species)/
  Burrowing Owl *Speotyto cunicularia*
Length 23-28 cm (9-11 in)

Further reading

Brown, L. H. *British Birds of Prey*. Collins,
London, 1976

Ford, Emma. *Birds of Prey*. Batsford, London, 1982

Hosking, E. & Flegg, J. *Eric Hosking's Owls*.
Pelham, London, 1982

Porter, R. & Holden, P. *Birds of Prey*. Usborne,
London, 1981

Saul, J. S. *Birds of Prey*. Granada, London, 1984

Sparks, J. & Soper, A. *Owls – their Natural and
Unnatural History*. David & Charles, Newton
Abbot, 1970

Wallace, Ian. *Birds of Prey in Britain and Europe*.
Oxford University Press, Oxford, 1983

Wardaugh, A. A. *Owls of Britain and Europe*.
Blandford, Poole, 1983

Weick, F. & Brown, L. H. *Birds of Prey of the
World*. Collins, London, 1980

INDEX

Numbers in *italics* refer to illustrations